CHAIRMAN BLAIR'S
LITTLE RED BOOK

Steve Bell
& Brian Homer

1 3 5 7 9 10 8 6 4 2

Published in 2001 by Methuen Publishing Ltd
215 Vauxhall Bridge Rd, London SW1V 1EJ

Written, Illustrated and Designed by Steve Bell & Brian Homer
Illustrations © 2001 by Steve Bell
Photographs © 2001 by Brian Homer

Methuen Publishing Limited Reg. No. 3543167

A CIP catalogue record for this book is available from the British Library

ISBN 0 413 76000 6

Printed and bound in Great Britain by
St Edmundsbury Press, Bury St Edmunds, Suffolk

CHAIRMAN BLAIR'S
LITTLE RED BOOK

Acknowledgements

Thanks to:
Heather Bell and Valerie Homer for their support and encouragement. Val for agreeing to be in the photographs without fully realising how they were going to be used! Max Eilenberg at Methuen for cutting-edge publishing and Thai lunches. Jane Bradish-Ellames for sterling agent efforts. Jim Deaves, Sue Race, Dave Harte and Will Bell for artwork assistance and Eleanor Rees at Methuen for copy editing.

Important note about use of quotations

The authors wish to make it clear that while many of Chairman Blair's sayings are reproduced verbatim in this volume, certain of his pronouncements have been written or improved in accordance with Third Way Thought. The latter bear the attribution '(Assisted)'.

CONTENTS

ABOUT THIS BOOK

Chairman Blair's Little Red Book is a guide for new practice. You will find that this book is most effective when waved rather than read.

When picking up the book, please take a moment to get the feel of its weight and suppleness. Grip the lower corners firmly between thumb and forefinger with your right hand. Give it a trial wave by raising it above your head and shaking it vigorously back and forth. This can be performed with both hands to lend extra emphasis.

When engaged in political discussion this book can be drawn out of the pocket swiftly and to great effect and will repel all doubters and sneering cynics.

Upon opening the book, feel the texture of the paper. Mmm! Rough, but not too rough. Words, but not too many. Pictures, just the right amount. Pages, quite a lot. Concepts, never more than one a page. Simple yet sophisticated. In short, a paean to Chairman Blair's every thought and deed.

To help beginners grasp the use of Chairman Blair's Little Red Book we include handy photo-story sections that indicate in graphic detail some of the wide ranges of uses of this small but highly effective book.

Advanced users will be able to develop their own uses for the book – and good luck to them.

Using Chairman Blair's Little Red Book No.1

Repelling a Sneering Cynic

Posed by models

1. Sneering cynic attacks

2. Defence with the Book

3. Making cynic eat his words

4. The Book takes effect

5. Victory is complete

FOREWORD TO THE THIRTEENTH EDITION

Colleague Anthony Charles Lynton Blair is the greatest Modernist-Social-ist of our era. He has invented, defended and developed Modernism-Social-ism with genius and creativity and has brought it to a higher and completely new stage in an era in which old-isms are heading for total collapse. It is a powerful weapon for opposing old-isms, rheumatism and running dogmatism.

Therefore, the most fundamental task in our Party's political work is to arm the minds of the people throughout the country with Chairman Blair's Thoughts and to persist in using them to command every field of activity.

In studying the works of Chairman Blair, one should have specific problems in mind. Study and apply his works in a creative way. Combine study with application. First study what must be urgently applied so as to get quick results, and strive hard to apply what one is studying.

We have compiled Chairman Blair's Little Red Book in order to help the massed colleagues learn Chairman Blair's thought more effectively.

It is our hope that all colleagues will earnestly learn and diligently bring about a new nationwide high tide in the creative study and application of Chairman Blair's works and strive to build our country into a great Modernist-Social-ist state with modern everything; with no running dogs and the trains running on time!

Jon Dog Du
April 1st, Dog Year 14007

LABOUR'S LEADER

Labour's Leader is Anthony Charles Lynton Blair, known respectfully to us all as Chairman Blair. He's the leader but he's humble. The current physical manifestation of Chairman Blair came into our world in 1953. But Blair's spirit is timeless and has been with us all since time immemorial.

At the appropriate age he went to school where he excelled in leadership with a human face. His school had no carpets which taught the young Blair a valuable lesson – always wear socks and if possible carry a spare pair.

At university he stood out because of his hard-drinkin', hard-rockin', church-goin' lifestyle. His verbless vocal delivery endeared him to his fanbase and he swung effortlessly on to the ladder of success.

His public school background was no impediment as he gravitated to the Party's northern heartland where he quickly became known as "Our Tony".

CHAIRMAN BLAIR'S LESSON No.1

"In today's world, there is no such thing as too clever. The more you know, the further you'll go."

Few of us are born with hair, fewer still with teeth, but Chairman Blair was launched into the world with both. No sooner had he been born than he was winning followers with his impish smile and coiffured good looks. He always had a ready gurgle for anyone who looked like they might be important.

This was a very new phenomenon, as most people were used to babies who snoozed, bawled and shat their pants. The fact that he was potty-trained from birth marked him out as an infant to be reckoned with. All who came into contact with him agreed that he was special, and it wasn't long before people were coming to him for advice, despite his lack of formal language skills. He became a focus for attention and was able to influence people's lives for the good with a startling vocabulary of grunts, farts and hand and ear gestures.

All this was a huge lesson for the nascent politician in him. He quickly realised that it was the essential newness in him that people were responding to. He never forgot this.

THE QUALITY OF NEWNESS

New is fresh.

New is clean.

New is unsullied.

New is for you.

New is for me.

Newness for all.

In the New Britain of the millennial frontier.

Britain today.

Let's face it.

Poor levels of newness.

We will raise levels of newness across the board.

We will eliminate non-newness by 2010.

How new are you?

How new are we?

How new is New Labour?

HOW NEW DO YOU WANT US TO BE?

How old is New Labour?

Chairman Blair was born in 1953, the Year of the Newt.

Chairman Blair became leader in 1994.

Chairman Blair is New Labour.

Labour became New Labour in 1994.

New Labour is seven in 2001.

Chairman Blair is ageless.

Happy birthday New Labour.

Every year another year.

Newness upon newness.

Year on year delivering newness to you.

THE LONG WALKIES No.1

My journey by J. Dog Du

It was Chairman Blair who first taught me the importance of political direction. At the time he was firmly towing me in a trolley behind his first bicycle. Today this bicycle can be seen in the Tate Blair Museum where colleagues may learn about his early influences.

In this way I had a salutary lesson in the meaning of left and right. That is to say I came to understand that left and right only made true sense in the wheel tracks of Chairman Blair's bicycle. I also learnt quite a lot about Chairman Blair's bottom because my trolley had no brakes. I therefore concluded that the future of transport lay in the proper implementation of the ancient art of Jaa Gwaa.

A FIFTIES AWAKENING

Chairman Blair put away childish things at the time of his birth. Though forced to wear short trousers, attend school and consume National Health orange juice, Chairman Blair was always Chairman Blair. Deprived of the opportunity to serve his nation in a military capacity by reason of the abolition of conscription and his extreme youth, he vowed that he would one day fulfil his destiny of service and leadership.

His early youth was punctuated with steam trains, trolley buses, Morris Minors and Austin A30s and the sound of traditional jazz, beatniks and brawling Teddy Boys. His political interest was stirred by the vacuum tubes and the divi at the local Co-op. This early manifestation of stakeholding excited him enormously. The way the money whizzed through the mysterious empty tubes to the accompaniment of loud sucking noises became a model for his ideological development.

Cold showers and the prospect of savage beatings also coloured his views and led him to long for a kinder, warmer, nicer, sort of non-confrontational and modern form of governance for all his fellows. The Tories always seemed to be in power and he conceived a desire to emulate them.

SIXTIES FLAIR

Chairman Blair liked the sixties. Old ideas were under challenge from newer ideas. Dull grey, tan and beige were swept away by fabrics of a more synthetic kind, made by man, with woman in mind. It was an exciting time and he found that his grin matched the brightness of the new, modernised fabrics. His trousers lengthened, then tightened as the decade progressed. Women in short skirts noticed his developing charms, but he was unflinching in his determination to make Britain great again.

Not for him the childish excesses of Jubblies and Wagon Wheels. He tasted them all once, but never swallowed. As the World Cup-winning goal bounced over the line Chairman Blair's thoughts turned to his impending departure for public school.

While the world outside went wild with demonstrations, flower power, love-ins and groovy music he had to be content with whatever comfort he could get from Matron. The "fagging" system made a deep impression on him. He vowed that when he achieved adulthood he would fight vigorously for the right of people to warm their own toilet seats.

CHAIRMAN BLAIR'S LESSON No.2

"I want to start where the British people start."

School taught Chairman Blair the importance of hierarchy and power. For all his small challenges to authority, he knew that in the end it was his destiny to become the man in charge. During his rebel months he flirted with the dangerous but essentially English music of Led Zeppelin and Cream, although he eventually broke with the former over their poor spelling. It was during this period that he learned to bang his head, but not too much, and to play air guitar, but not while anyone else was watching.

He tried his hand at songwriting. His first effort, catchily entitled *I want to start where the British People start*, sank without trace, but he was able to re-use it to great effect in his speech to his loyal followers at Bournemouth in 1999.

Despite the harsh discipline at this exclusive and expensive school, it was here that the words of Rudyard Kipling found an echo in his youthful breast:

If you can talk with crowds and keep your virtue,

Or walk with Kings – nor lose the common touch...

THE PLEASURES OF DISCIPLINE

"Look at Britain. Great strengths. Great history. English, the language of the new technology. The national creative genius of the British people. But wasted."

Chairman Blair's speech was not always as immaculately verbless as it is today. His school years were instrumental in purging verbs almost entirely from his linguistic palate. Early on in his school career, when challenged by a master to explain his behaviour, it would often be ten minutes or more before he got to the point. This usually had the master spluttering, "Spit it out boy!" accompanied by a swift board rubber in the ear.

Experience taught him to eliminate verbs in order to get his point across. A small fragment of one of his explanations has been preserved for posterity and is now held in a vacuum-sealed vault at the Tate Blair Museum in Greenwich.

EARLY EFFORTS AT PRUDENCE

Chairman Blair first met the boy who would be not quite king but who would prove to be a staunch ally and close personal friend in Scotland. When still quite young he started attending the services of an obscure minority Christian sect called the Wee Free Bankers of Scotland.

The minister at the church was the father of an earnest and stocky young lad called G'Dong Bru. The minister himself was a stern and unforgiving man with uncompromising views on religious prudence and saving for a rainy day in a sock under the mattress. His name was Robert the Bru but his reputation was so fearsome that he was called Iron Bru (but never to his face).

The most striking thing about G'Dong Bru himself was the way in which the young lad seemed to have absorbed his father's fiery determination to remain prudent at all costs. He was fond of repeating ad nauseam favourite sayings of his father:

"Dinnae tak onny wooden money, sonny."
"Porridge is highly nourishing but maks puir wallpaper paste."
"A poond in the haund is worth three by Tuesday."

With this fabulous grounding in economic reality, how could G'Dong Bru fail to become in later life Bru the Iron Chancellor? Chairman Blair, of course, could see this at a glance, and he made sure that G'Dong Bru was initiated into his group of close confidants and pets, where he remains to this day.

IRON BRU

G'DONG BRU

THE LIGHT OF OUR LIVES

"Don't get me wrong, I believe in God, but here on earth,
Leaders still have to lead..."
(Assisted)

Chairman Blair shines his light on us all. Wherever we may
be and whatever we are doing his light gets through to us.
We feel its penetrating rays. We feel its warming glow. It
sustains and nourishes our every thought and deed. It gives
us strength to persevere when all around us are shouting
that we have made a mistake. Not for us the easy way out
of a swift apology – for it is our duty to correct the wrong
thinking of the criticisers and to bring them back into the
full glory of his light.

We, his loyal followers, have his light to lean on, but where,
you may ask, does Chairman Blair get his strength? From
within is the answer. Yet there is a part of him that is but
a receptacle for the One who has pretensions to even greater
newness than our leader. He goes by many names in many
cultures but for Chairman Blair there is but one Bigger
Cheese (BC) than him – the Almighty himself.

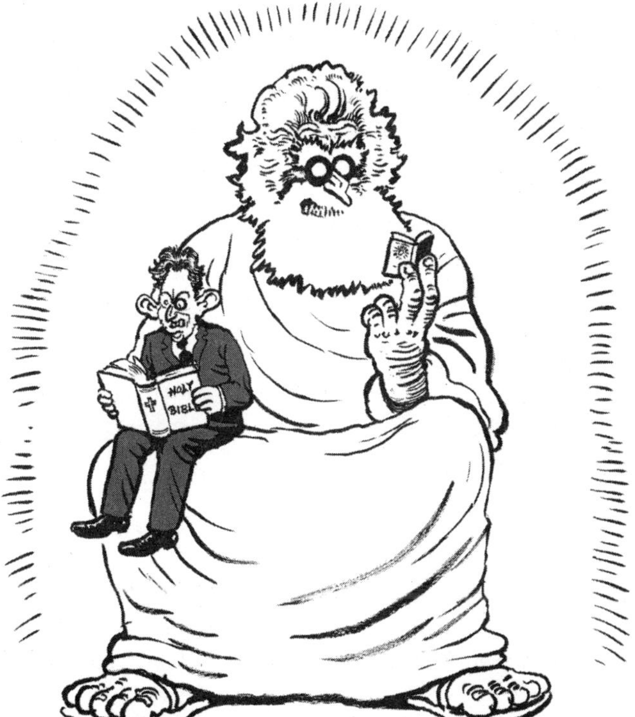
HOLY
BIBL

THE LONG WALKIES No.2

My journey by J. Dog Du

My first experience of modern high speed travel was in the baggage car on the East Coast Express to Edinburgh on the way with Chairman Blair to his new school.

The driver had kicked me out of the cab and no amount of whining at Chairman Blair's feet would persuade him to take up my case.

"We must always save our energies for battles that we can win," said the surprisingly coherent and studious Young Leader as he carried me in my new containment unit to the baggage car.

"Look, good place, here," he said kindly and added, "Stay, walkies soon. Edinburgh."

It was at this point that I realised that I would never get to occupy the driver's seat. My duty was to be ever at the side of Chairman Blair and to help him fulfil his destiny.

OUR HEROIC LEADER No. 2:
VOWING NEVER TO WARM ANYBODY'S TOILET SEAT
EVER AGAIN.

SEVENTIES CHANGE

The seventies were a time of change for Chairman Blair. His appetite for extra work gained him a place at St John's College, Oxford to read Law. He was intellectually restless and a voracious reader. But he was somehow unsatisfied.

His first attempts at achieving satisfaction were in the field of "rock" music. As Chairman Blair has said himself, "I have always been 'crazy' about 'rock' music." He became lead singer of the "Not Too Naughty Boys", a combo renowned for its modest cover versions of such classics as "My Mojo's on the Blink" and "F*** me, F***-face 'til I Fart."

But this foray into the world of sex, no drugs and rock and roll left him still unfulfilled. He needed stimulation of a different kind. Something that would assuage his spiritual and social hunger.

It was then that he met the plain-talking, hard-drinking, god-bothering Johnny O'Pope, a distant relative of the Pontiff. This unpredictable and charismatic character opened Chairman Blair's mind to the need to reconcile radical social change with the need to get "bums on pews".

He was also captivated by the ideas of the obscure Scottish philosopher Jimmy "Hardman" McKnox, author of such works as "See us a Poond 'til Tuesday, Oh Lordy" and "The Glasgow Kiss: A Philosopher's View."

His head became filled with new thought. The possibilities seemed endless – particularly to his friends. They were impressed, though not in any positive sense, by his sudden outpourings of piousness and preaching – often after nights spent quaffing Hirondelle and smoking other people's Player's No.6.

From purely selfish motives his friends encouraged him to undertake a Mission to spread the good word up the Tees. This turned out to be a short trip and by most people's standards a bit of a disaster. However, for Chairman Blair it was an early chance to redefine the concept of defeat, as expressed in the contemporary Bob Dylan lyric, "There's no success like failure."

CHAIRMAN BLAIR'S LESSON No.3

"We hold firm. We listen and we lead."

University taught Chairman Blair that in order to lead you need to be in a position to lead. It is something that requires a great deal of preparation, and that process is a lifelong journey.

By getting an Oxford education he put himself on the fast track to Leadership, for many are called but few are chosen, and those few generally come from Oxford or Cambridge.

THE MISSION UP THE TEES

Chairman Blair does not talk much about his Mission Up the Tees. The facts are shrouded in an evil-smelling chemical fog. Research has unearthed a version of what actually happened.

Apparently he arrived at Middlesbrough station one dark and dank Wednesday in November of 1974, full of desperate optimism. His stay would not last long.

He selected one of the fifty-two Working Men's Clubs adjacent to the station. Inside he discovered drunken taciturn men with pigeons on their heads and whippets at their sides discussing the tactical formation Boro would require in order to succeed in their cup run.

With his long hair, tank top and flared trousers, he didn't need to say anything to attract attention. In the ensuing silence he made his move. As he lunged in panic for the door, a pint pot caught him a glancing blow on the back of his head, while a whippet made away with the back of his trousers.

Despite the qualified success of his Mission Up the Tees, the heady mix of alcohol, piss, cigarette smoke and religion engendered in Chairman Blair a passion for northern politics that has remained with him ever since.

Back in Oxford he watched with growing alarm as Trade Unionists drinking beer and eating sandwiches began to hold the country to ransom. He realised the error of the Old Labour ways and began to see the civilising potential of a nice bottle of Chianti and a few exotic nibbles.

He was disturbed by the continuing economic upheaval of the late seventies and was politically aroused by the rise to power of Ma Gra Tha Tcha.

Using Chairman Blair's Little Red Book No.2

Backing up political points with the Little Red Book

Posed by models

Take that, you Forces of Conservatism!

1.

2.

3.

4.

CHAIRMAN BLAIR AND THE OPPOSITE SEX

Chairman Blair was what is now called a "babe magnet". Women flocked to his side, attracted by his classic manly looks. He was vastly tall with piercing blue eyes and loose, rangy, athletic limbs. This, combined with his strangely squinty countenance, his weak chin and his protruding lower lip and enormous ears, made him irresistible to women.

During Chairman Blair's time at university Oxford became a Mecca for young women. They came from all directions just to be near him. They came from the North, they came from the South, they came from above, they came from below, they even came from abroad. They came from the trees, they came from the hills and they didn't care.

It was amazing that he graduated at all, given the time he had to spend fighting women off. Even his college-supplied shitty stick failed to keep them away.

At "Not Too Naughty Boys" gigs the amplified band could scarcely be heard above the caterwauling and shrieking of his nubile young admirers. His lead singing was fortunately rarely heard either.

THE NEWNESS OF YOUTH

When Chairman Blair graduated he was still an extremely young man, though his spirit was eternal. For him the world was a fresh place, full of limitless choices and opportunities. Young women quite literally threw themselves at him while old men were happy to sit at his feet. In short, what he had was the magnetism of youth, a quality in him that remains as strong as ever today.

He realised that his search for meaning was actually getting in the way of looking mean, which in the language of the time meant looking groovy or hip. Part of Chairman Blair's breakthrough was in discarding old and useless values like "meaning" and introducing new and impressive values of delivery, phraseology and clean teeth. Some say that he was the true progenitor of the "soundbite".

Moving into the profession of the Law involved moving into dark suits and occasional casual wear with a hint of the formal – no denim ever unpressed – which has remained his core wardrobe value ever since.

THE LONG WALKIES No.3

My journey by J. Dog Du

My career at sea began on the prow of a punt on the Cherwell in Oxford. Chairman Blair was expertly poling us along while his latest glamorous conquest lounged on cushions sipping her babycham from his shoe.

Generous as ever, Chairman Blair tossed me tasty morsels to eat. Unfortunately these kept falling into the water. This taught me that you might give food to a dog on a punt but it will still get a good ducking.

LAW STUDIES

The young newly-qualified Chairman Blair had absolutely no problem in gaining a pupillage at one of the top chambers in the land. Da Ree Ur Vin, the florid and charismatic QC who was Head of Chambers, was immediately bowled over by the sheer brilliance of the young legal talent.

Chairman Blair was a natural at the law. With his clear-eyed stare and his devastating legal arguments he transfixed judge, jury, witnesses and defendants alike. His appetite for detail and his capacity for sheer hard work meant that he never put a foot wrong. He never lost a case or even a plastic bag.

In his first year as a barrister he made so much money that he was able to prepare the way for his later political forays by buying up an entire terrace of houses in a northern town, including the occupants – one of whom just happened to be a senior local councillor.

This man, Pee Pan Joh, was to prove one of Chairman Blair's staunchest allies in his relentless pursuit of a safe Labour seat. He saw the glamorous young man's potential as a political lion who would stand up to the bully boys of the hard left.

CHAIRMAN BLAIR – THE MAN

Chairman Blair is not interested in power for its own sake, but simply to further his own ends. He is always surprisingly calm, reasonable and approachable, except when someone or something has incurred his displeasure, when he can be critical, but his firmness is always fair, and his fairness is always firm. Jon Dog Du has personal experience of this:

"I had an unfortunate accident at the conference in 1994 and Chairman Blair had no hesitation in whipping out a plastic bag and sparing my blushes. It was a very warm, human gesture which I have never forgotten and he will never let me forget."

Many colleagues want to know what Chairman Blair is really like. It is no exaggeration to say that he towers above ordinary men (and women) but not by too much. It is a modest amount of towering.

He is incapable of allowing his intellect to intimidate. It is almost incredible how he refuses the trappings of power. Not for him the excesses of old. For example, his Prime Ministerial Jaa Gwaa is not quite top of the range. It lacks

the heated seat, because he knows that at the bottom of his appeal is the coolness of his bottom.

He is clever but not too clever, intelligent but not too intelligent, witty but not too witty. His judgement is impeccable but not too impeccable. He likes cats but not too many cats. He is humble but not too humble. He has thoughts but not too many. He is human but...

He has a certain steely vulnerability which women find attractive; he's stiff but not too stiff. His clothes fit well yet they are modest. Not for him the sartorial excesses of an Emperor Bokassa. He is happy to dress casually in order to make others feel at ease in his company. For example he has never insisted that anyone purchase a tie before entering Number Ten.

He treats colleagues as equals, but not too equal. He has an easy air of informality, except with those he cannot stand. He suffers fools but not too gladly.

CHAIRMAN BLAIR'S LESSON No.4

"I lead to serve. You serve to lead. To service the leadership. That is your aim."
(Assisted)

Chairman Blair has fond memories of the moment he committed himself to lead and serve. It was a wet Westminster Wednesday outside, but inside it was as warm and bright as a Tuscan Tuesday afternoon by the pool. The stunning neo-gothic setting of the Palace of Westminster struck Chairman Blair dumb for the first and only time in his life.

As the young twenty-seven-year-old sat in the huge central lobby surrounded by larger than life-sized statues of politicians from bygone ages, he realised he had only one choice to secure his place in history. Politics was his only option, to lead was his destiny. He looked around immediately for somebody to vote for him. It was at that moment that his eyes lit upon U Toe Dee MP who was to introduce him to the arcane workings of the Old Labour hierarchy.

U Toe Dee was instantly impressed by the young man's carriage, bearing and gleaming smile. Later he was to tell friends: "This boy will go far. He has the teeth and ears for it. I would say it's a toss-up, but on the whole I think the ears have it, the ears have it."

CHAIRMAN BLAIR MEETS CHA REE BOO

It was at the chambers of Da Ree Ur Vin that Chairman Blair met the blazing legal talent of Cha Ree Boo, who was as beautiful as she was talented. From the beginning it was obvious to everyone that this was a match made in heaven.

Cha Ree Boo was always destined to succeed from the moment she was born into the theatrical Boo dynasty. Her father was the revered and sonorous Sir Ya Boo, star of such cultural gems as the long-running saga "Confucius was a Window Cleaner".

The whole Boo family were feted and lauded throughout the land and included such luminaries as her sister Pee Ka Boo as well as her less well-known brother Hoo Boo and her distant and estranged cousin Boo Boo.

Witnesses speak of a strong electrical discharge at the moment of their meeting over a hot brief in Da Ree Ur Vin's chambers. The lights flickered, never to come on again in our time because this gilded couple would shortly become the source of all power.

CHA REE BOO

LIFE IN ISLINGTON:
THE BALSAMIC YEARS

The Blair–Boo marriage was something to behold. Figures from the worlds of law, politics and entertainment came to pay court to the handsome young pair. Da Ree Ur Vin, in a memorable speech, described them as "the gleaming grin on the future face of Britain". Their honeymoon was on the Tuscan estate of Prince Dom Inazione Con Trollata, the tanned and brilliant young inventor of balsamic vinegar.

North London was an ideal place for Chairman Blair, with Cha Ree Boo at his side, to map out his road to power. It began in Hackney and led via Drayton Park to Islington, and thence inevitably to Downing Street itself.

But first Chairman Blair had to hone his dietary skills. When he first came to the capital he had never heard of a sun-dried tomato. Like most people at that time he believed that tomatoes grew in tins, or possibly sauce bottles. Where he came from there was never enough sun to dry one anyway.

Islington was a gateway to a cornucopia of gastronomic possibilities. From all-night guacamole bars to the Polish Food Centre it throbbed and sizzled with the overpowering smell of hot spicy food in unusual combinations. The young couple were instrumental in bringing the pleasures of balsamic vinegar to a North London hungry for new cult food, and very soon became involved in organising the 'Beating the Balsam' Festival among the local community.

THE LONG WALKIES No.4

My journey by J. Dog Du

Moving to London was an exciting introduction to a whole new world of public transport possibilities. The Underground, or 'tube' as it is known locally, was a revelation. Deep holes in the ground full of people and not a rabbit to be seen anywhere.

At first Chairman Blair was unsettled by the signs at the top of the moving staircases, or "escalators", which said "Dogs Must Be Carried". He thought it a severe infringement of his personal liberty to be forced to carry a heavy dog like me in order to travel on the Underground.

Later when he discovered his mistake he administered a vigorous kick to my behind to express his relief and thanks.

DOGS
MUST BE
CARRIED

OUR HEROIC LEADER No.4:
REVELATION IN THE PALACE
OF WESTMINSTER

DISCOVERING THE THIRD WAY

"My generation stands at the intersection between old and new."

In the early eighties the Old Labour Party had fallen into the hands of the extreme left faction led by the slavering rene- gade Toe Nee Ben, though the then leader was the enfeebled former firebrand Ol Mik Foo (with his dog Dee Zee). Chairman Blair's talents were widely recognised throughout the Party, but few realised his true potential. Some even laughed at the apparently chinless young lawyer with the cheesy smile. Later they would bitterly regret this false thinking.

In 1982, at the height of Ma Gra Tha Tcha's triumph in the Falklands, the safe Tory seat of Beaconsfield became vacant. Labour's prospects seemed hopeless, but young Chairman Blair succeeded in coming third and losing his deposit against all the odds. This triumph came at the right time to encourage him on to even greater heights and brought him to the attention of the Old Labour leadership. Ol Mik Foo was bowled over by this thrusting young man.

Beaconsfield was also significant in that it was here that Chairman Blair discovered the Third Way whilst crossing the busy A40 in the middle of town.

Beaconsfield stands at the intersection between Slough and High Wycombe and Gerrards Cross and Amersham, between South and North Bucks, where the old A40 is intersected by the A355, yet where the new M40 has largely replaced the old A40 as a major trunk route. The New has replaced the Old but the Old still remains, distinctive, characterful, redundant, yet in some ways enhanced by the reduction of traffic.

This inspired Chairman Blair and he saw that there was a way that was neither left nor right, up nor down, across nor not across, in nor out, north nor south, east nor west. It is easy to imagine but hard to find. Only Chairman Blair has been able to put his finger or foot on it.

This was a seminal moment. He felt as if he alone stood on the precise intersection between the Old and the New. He was the fulcrum, the handle, the lever, indeed the big knob. From now on he was going to be at the centre of everything. From him would flow the changes that would need to be made to the Party and the Country. The world could wait for a little bit longer.

SOCIALISM AND SOCIAL-ISM

"The rich man in his castle, the poor man at his gate: it won't wash any more."

Old Labour's continued failure to win elections during the 1980s troubled Chairman Blair, particularly after his discovery of the Third Way. How could the electorate continue to reject a Party with him in it? Only he had the vision clear enough to see what the British People really needed, and only he was equipped to deliver it.

The problem with Socialism was that it was too left wing. Using Third Way Thinking Chairman Blair identified the problem. All it needed was a simple hyphen. This would separate the 'Social' from the 'ism', creating a whole new 'ism' that was neither left nor right, up nor down, across nor not across, in nor out, north nor south, east nor west. His new concept was Social-ism.

This was an 'ism' for all our People. This was the one true unifying 'ism' of the modern age. It would be all the 'ism' that anybody would ever need.

CORRECTING MISTAKEN IDEAS

Mistaken ideas were rife during the 1980s within the Old Labour Party. Chairman Blair's task was to get everybody thinking New Third Way Thoughts. Only constant reference back to the core values of the Third Way would enable mistaken ideas to be isolated and cauterised from the body of the Party. Many had tried, but only a few of his inner coterie were fully able on their own to comprehend the Third Way and to apply it effectively. Success could only be achieved through the medium of Chairman Blair.

His advice to all who aspire to serve him is simple. Take your thoughts and deeds, rigorously review them in the light of the Third Way, and then repeat the Third Way inwardly.

You will find that after several hours you will be unable to remember your original mistaken ideas or deeds. You will find that you will have grasped Chairman Blair's Little Red Book and you will be holding it to your chest and you will be thinking only pure Third Way Thoughts.

NewMullet
NewLabour

The **Third** Way

To be repeated as often as necessary and more

Neither left nor right

Neither up nor down

Neither across nor not across

Neither in nor out

Neither north nor south

Neither east nor west

CHAIRMAN BLAIR'S LESSON No.5

"I know this... from 'New' Labour... that the 'new' was necessary in order to 're-new' the old."

The moment of revelation while crossing the A40 in Beaconsfield was the very intersection between his old life as schoolboy, student, barrister and young married person and his new life as Chairman Blair. It was here, in effect, that he became Chairman Blair as we now know him, even though he was not actually to become Leader of the Labour Party for another twelve years.

Some say it is a miracle that the young Chairman Blair was not knocked down and killed, distracted as he was by the sudden overpowering revelation of the Third Way. Other, wiser heads understand that no power on earth, be it earthquake, bus or articulated lorry, could have ever come between Chairman Blair and his destiny.

CRITICISM AND SELF-CRITICISM

"...Neil Kinnock, wasn't it brilliant yesterday?"

The 1983 election on the surface marked something of a low point for the Labour Party. It received its lowest share of the popular vote since 1918. More significantly, however, it marked the arrival of Chairman Blair in Parliament as member for the new constituency of Clogthwaite-on-Tees, which knew a good thing when it saw it.

Chairman Blair's instinctive understanding of the people and culture of Clogthwaite meant that the area became a springboard for the mass movement that would turn Third Way theory into glorious practice. He proposed a revolutionary project whereby people could become Labour Party members even if they'd never heard of the Labour Party.

NEE KEE NOK

Suddenly Party meetings became social occasions. Clogthwaite was introduced to such exciting and unheard-of concepts as guacamole and balsamic vinegar. A "Beating The Balsam North" Festival was introduced to universal acclaim.

Yet before Chairman Blair could fulfil his destiny, the Labour Party had to become New, and before Labour could become New it had to be purged of that which was Old. Nee Kee Nok and Ha Ta Slee, an erstwhile left-wing Welsh oratorical firebrand and a fat bloke from Sheffield, were well suited to this task.

HA TA SLEE

Together they took on the forces around the slavering renegade Toe Nee Ben, the Trotskyist Lesbian Schemers of Mi Li Tant, and other assorted ideological detritus and swept them out of the Party and into eternal irrelevance.

Meanwhile, the monstrous imperialist reactionary Ma Gra Tha Tcha and her henchman Wun Fat Blip were wreaking havoc on the economy and workforce of the British Isles, imposing their own Third Way measures without understanding their true significance. A whirlwind was being sown, without the instinctive sympathy that Chairman Blair would later bring to the same role. Theirs was a corrupted and perverse version of the Third Way:

"Neither left nor left; neither east nor east; and Get Orff My Land!"

WUN FAT BLIP

Old**Labour**   New**Labour**

Old**Labour**	New**Labour**
Keir Hardie	Kir Royale
Chairman Mao	Ciao
Facial Hair	Hair and Facial
Charabanc	People Carrier
Socialist Realism	Realistic Social-ism
Clause Four	4X4
Woodbine and a Pint of Mild	Stick of Celery and a Glass of Water
Mushy Peas	Guacamole
Joined-up Writing	Joined-up Thinking
Codpiece	Monkfish in Raspberry Coulis

THE ONE-EYED TROUSER SNAKE

It was on a pilgrimage to dance on Karl Marx's grave in Highgate Cemetery that Chairman Blair first came upon Man Dee, the all-seeing, all-knowing and ever so slightly supercilious media manipulator and one-eyed trouser snake. Man Dee was wrapped around a tree adjacent to the grave of the great but wrong-thinking political thinker. Man Dee's first words were: "Did you know my grandfather? He was famous in the Labour Party, as I intend to be."

Chairman Blair replied: "Not if I get there first, snake features." In spite of this initial prickliness, a firm bond was established between the pair from that moment on.

Man Dee had a special gift for crushing opponents' arguments by swallowing them whole, digesting them and then regurgitating them in perfect Third Way form. Chairman Blair had found a true political soulmate who instinctively understood the depth of Third Way thinking and was able to apply it consistently to any situation.

On comparing notes, they discovered that Chairman Blair had had the Third Way revealed to him a good ten minutes before Man Dee, and that therefore he could claim to be the senior partner in the enterprise.

THE LONG WALKIES No.5

My journey by J. Dog Du

When I first heard that Chairman Blair was taking me out to a Thai Restaurant I thought I was in for a full slap-up feed.

Imagine my disappointment when I ended up tied to a lamp post outside a trendy Islington Eatery while Chairman Blair and that one-eyed trouser snake Man Dee caroused with all the movers and shakers late into the night.

I realised that this was not a disappointment but another opportunity to learn humility on my path to Third Way enlightenment.

OUR HEROIC LEADER No.5
THE CLASS WAR IS OVER

Using Chairman Blair's Little Red Book No.3

Discovering the Third Way
Posed by models

1. Reading

2. Contemplating

3. Discussing

4. Finding

5. Pre-realisation

6. Realisation

7. Confirmation

8. Communication

THE BIRTH OF THE RED MULLET

Old Labour had an image problem. It looked old, stale and stained. What was needed was a fresh young attractive look, a look that would make people say, "Hey, have you seen the Labour Party recently?"

The 55,000-strong communications team set to work immediately. They tried all sorts of new symbols. The Gladiolus was quickly discarded, along with the Chrysanthemum, the Venus Fly Trap and the Toadstool.

Of course it was Chairman Blair himself who realised that they were on the wrong track. It was not the plant kingdom but the animal kingdom – in fact, Fish – that should be the inspiration. So it was that Chairman Blair created the powerful new concept of the Red Mullet of Social-ism. Many many versions of the Red Mullet were tried until Chairman Blair himself picked up the pencil and drew the version that we all know today.

It was during the 1987 election that the Red Mullet of Social-ism was first deployed to great effect. Who can forget such memorable slogans as:

This is the authentic
Red Mullet of Social-ism

"Mullet Over – Vote Labour"
and
"Red Dawn, Red Mullet".

Thanks to these and
other slogans conceived
by the dream team of Chairman Blair
and Man Dee, Labour was able,
against all the odds, to storm to
a well-deserved second place.
With this success behind
them they were able to
look forward with con-
fidence to the next
election.

Get the graphics people to sharpen this up
Tony Blair
(Chairman-in-waiting)

LIFE IN ISLINGTON: THE SUSHI YEARS

After the success of the Balsamic Years, the Blair Boo family were not disposed to rest on their laurels. They diligently applied themselves to new culinary heights. This period would later become known as "The Sushi Years".

Raw fish was to be an abiding theme of Chairman Blair's ascent to the apex of power. As he said at the time:

"It's time to choose: Labour is neither fish nor fowl. I say make it Fish!" (Assisted)

His 1988 trip to the Dogger Bank with Jon Dog Du confirmed him in this view. On this visit Chairman Blair was moved by the response he got when he addressed the waves:

"I am a unifier, a builder of consensus. I don't believe in sloppy compromise. But I do believe in bringing people and fish together." (only slightly Assisted)

Witnesses of this keynote speech swear to this day that above the noise of the wind and the waves they could hear the thunderous applause of a passing shoal of cod.

CHAIRMAN BLAIR'S LESSON No.6

The monstrous imperialist reactionary Ma Gra Tha Tcha was continuing to impose her own corrupted and perverse version of the Third Way causing widespread havoc.

Nonetheless Chairman Blair had always been secretly impressed by the style and power of her leadership. He didn't agree with all her policies, but what particularly impressed him was her ability to sweep aside opposing points of view.

He first felt her raw power whilst sitting opposite her on the opposition front bench in the House of Commons. Their stares met across a crowded chamber and he felt a warm glow. He then realised that he had pissed his pants for the first time in several decades.

He could only watch in admiration tinged with a hint of eroticism as she tore Nee Kee Nok limb from limb in front of him. It was all he could do to stop himself from joining in.

He realised that it was power, not policy, that really turned him on. He made a mental note to encourage Cha Ree Boo to wear more blue with cast iron accessories in future.

THE WRONG ROAD TO VICTORY

Ma Gra Tha Tcha became increasingly unpopular and the
cardboard running dog lackeys of the
Conservative Party engineered her
removal from office. She was replaced as
Party leader by a laughable nonentity
called Joh Ma Ja and everything
seemed set fair for a Labour victory in 1992. The slogans were
in place, the Red Mullet was in
place and the triumphalism was
in place. Unfortunately for the
Labour Party the wrong
leader was in place. The
hapless Nee Kee Nok
was no Chairman
Blair. He had
neither the hair,
the ears nor the
teeth, nor the
sheer hunger and
will to use them on
his political enemies.

JOH MA JAA

104

For the fourth time in a row the Labour Party came a heroic second. Nee Kee Nok was so shagged out that he resigned in ignominy. Unfortunately for the Labour Party, as Leader Blair awaited the call from the massed colleagues to rescue the party, a short bald and portly Scotsman with glasses came out of nowhere to seize the leadership. This man, Joh Smee, represented the cuddly wing of the party.

He charmed his way into the hearts of party members by doing very little very well and simply looking on while the discredited Joh Ma Ja regime fell apart. Sadly this was not enough, and he died in 1994. The country ground to a halt as people from all sides of the political spectrum fought with each other to pay ever more glowing personal tributes to the statesmanship of this remarkably short, bald, portly and Scottish politician whose like we would never see again until Do Na Du Waa died six years later, though he wasn't as portly, nor nearly as bald.

JOH SMEE

SELF-RELIANCE
AND ARDUOUS STRUGGLE

To be Leader one needs to lead. A struggle to lead, a struggle to rely, a struggle to struggle. The sense of struggle is a struggle against sense, where sense becomes the enemy and the only thing on which one can rely is struggle.

The struggle to modernise the Labour Party, which Chairman Blair undertook as soon as he became Leader of that Party was, in a sense, just such a struggle against sense. Through struggle he successfully transcended the Party and became the Party.

The struggle is the Party, and now the Party is the struggle. The struggle is to join, and to join is to struggle, but it should not be a struggle to join the Party. "I am sorry, all our agents are busy," is not a response we wish to give. We must struggle to install more phone lines, but on the other hand the struggle to get through will only be beneficial to the strugglers for it is only through struggle that one can truly be said to have joined.

CORRECT IDEAS

Where do correct ideas come from? Do they drop from the skies? No. Are they innate in the mind? No. They come from the Third Way, and from it alone; they come from three kinds of Third Way, the First Third Way, the Second Third Way and the Third Third Way.

Some people ask what are these Ways. But, as Chairman Blair would say: if you don't already know, why are you asking?

Generally speaking, ideas that succeed are correct and ideas that fail are incorrect.

Often, correct ideas can be arrived at only after many repetitions of the process leading from matter to consciousness and then back to matter, that is, leading from practice to ideas and then back to practice. Such is the Third Way theory of knowledge, the Modernist Social-ist theory of knowledge.

THE LONG WALKIES No.6

My journey by J. Dog Du

My first experience of flying was when young Chairman Blair hurled me from an upper window at school to see if I could. My first experience in an aeroplane was when Chairman Blair and I went on a fact-finding visit to see how they dealt with unwanted pregnancies among unmarried dogs in Northern Canada.

Instead of first class, Chairman Blair insisted that I travel in the unheated baggage hold in order to guard his important Third Way archive material being prepared for his teams of biographers, who even before his ascension to ultimate power were clamouring to tell his story. This experience taught me the valuable lesson that no matter how high you fly, your knackers are still going to get frozen off.

SEIZING THE MOMENT

In 1994 Chairman Blair was able effortlessly to win the leadership election and to turn tired Old Labour into young thrusting New Labour instantaneously at one and the same time. Opposition melted away like snow in the sun under the force of his towering intellect.

The Red Mullet of Social-ism sucked up everything in its path like a python eating an antelope. Nothing was safe. Whole rafts of reactionary ideology were swallowed whole, including Ah Wee Coo's bloomers and Joh Ma Ja's underpants. From this moment, like babies left naked on a bare mountain, the Tories were doomed. The Red Mullet of Social-ism turned a remarkable and satisfying shade of turquoise.

All that remained now was for Chairman Blair's enterprise to be crowned with the ultimate and inevitable prize of first place in a General Election.

113

THE NEW LABOUR PARTY

New Labour is not an easy party to describe. We live in new times and the New Labour Party sets new standards. Gone are the days of old standards and Austin Sevens. Now is the time for new wheels and new thinking. New Labour provides that thinking in abundance.

New paragraph. Understanding New Labour is one thing, but the harder task of getting to grips with New Labour depends on understanding that, in giving renewed expression to newness (see Page 152), New Labour is newer than Old Labour.

New Labour is different from Old Labour in many other ways, not least in its stratagems for power. New Labour understands that power flows from a power station and that the closer you are to the source of power, the better the chance of ending up in charge.

New History will record the remarkable transformation of the Labour Party under Chairman Blair, a transformation that is chronicled by his thoughts. For he is our leader (see Page 13) and as such has the responsibility of leadership (see Page 106)

Traditional values...

...in a modern
setting

DARE TO RELAX, DARE TO WIN

Chairman Blair leads an exceptional life which is at the same time utterly normal. He lives each minute to the full and packs a lot into each minute. Ordinary people live from minute to minute but Chairman Blair has a strategy for each minute which is planned years in advance.

What would take a normal person one hour, Chairman Blair can achieve in one minute. Because there are sixty minutes in an hour, the Scientific Third Way shows us that Chairman Blair can do sixty things at once.

Of course, being a woman, Cha Ree Boo can actually do three hundred and sixty things at once. Fortunately for Chairman Blair, two hundred and forty of these are taken up by the legal cases she is simultaneously undertaking while the other one hundred and twenty are taken up with preparing her extensive wardrobe in order to entertain visiting Heads of State.

Of necessity Chairman Blair has other people to struggle for him while he keeps an eye on the Bigger Picture. Chairman Blair has found that the most effective way to keep an eye on the Bigger Picture is to take a Po Waa Cat Nap.

The Po Waa Cat Nap should last a minimum of three minutes and a maximum of seventeen hours. This ensures that Chairman Blair is the most relaxed of leaders and yet ready to spring at a moment's notice into steely and determined action.

CHAIRMAN BLAIR'S LESSON 7

"I am a unifier but I have an irreducible core within me..."

As Chairman Blair later revealed, the key to his success was the discovery of his "irreducible core". One evening while he and Cha Ree Boo were in the bath cleansing themselves to be ready for a new day of leadership, Cha Ree Boo exclaimed: "What's that?" To which Chairman Blair replied:

"My God, I seem to have an irreducible core! Who would have thought it after all these years. Come Cha Ree, help me! We must make sure it never ever boils away!"

119

CORRECT BEHAVIOUR
ON BATTLEBUSES

Chairman Blair began the general election campaign in the spring of 1997 in the certain knowledge that he would triumph. This was no shallow triumphalism born of insecurity, as had been the case with the pathetically eager figure of Nee Kee Nok in 1992. Rather it was a confident certainty based on a true and clear Third Way understanding of the forces that shape New History.

Despite this knowledge Chairman Blair always took pains to emphasise to his followers and colleagues that "this is no time for complacency." This was not hypocrisy on Chairman Blair's part, but a statement of a fundamental political truth. Chairman Blair is eternally vigilant to the fact that even the best laid plans can be liable to a reduced success factor through the misunderstanding and incorrect thinking of even the closest colleagues.

Therefore, all colleagues and journalists should carefully observe the rules set out on the following pages when campaigning on battlebuses.

New**Mullet**
New**Labour**

Instructions to **Colleagues** on **Battlebuses**

Colleagues must be sober.
Colleagues must be clean.
Colleagues must be clean shaven.
Colleagues must be soberly dressed.
Colleagues must be thoroughly versed in
    Third Way Thought.
Colleagues must never take drugs.
Colleagues must eat Raw Fish at least
    once a week.
Colleagues must be polite.
Colleagues must be prepared to struggle with every
    fibre of their being for the Leader.

NewMullet
NewLabour

Instructions to Journalists on Battlebuses

Journalists should be sober.

Journalists should be clean.

Journalists should be clean shaven.

Journalists should refrain from awkward or indelicate questions at all times.

Journalists should never denigrate the precepts of Third Way Thought.

Journalists should be flexible.

Journalists should be helpful.

Journalists should be prepared at any hour of the day or night to receive special briefings from Chairman Blair.

THE FORCES OF CONSERVATISM ARE CARDBOARD DOGS

The absolutely incontrovertible truth of Third Way Thought makes any opposition futile. Since the Conservative Party got rid of the monstrous imperialist Ma Gra Tha Tcha, who despite her many failings and disastrous record did at least possess a faint glimmer of insight into the Third Way, it has been a hollow Party, a Party of Ghosts and Shades, a Party of Cardboard Dogs. This is well expressed in one of Chairman Blair's favourite sayings:

"If Cardboard Dogs could piss they would become mulch on the pathway to the Third Way all the sooner."
(Assisted)

OldLabour	**New**Labour	
White Heat of Technology	The Power of the Internet	
Red Hot and Dutch	Duchy Originals	
Short Back and Sides	Short Sides and Back	
Brylcreem	Styling Mousse	
Ferrets	Chinchillas	
Newts	One-eyed Trouser Snakes	
Beer and Sandwiches	Chianti and Ciabatta	
Comrade	Colleague	
Flat Cap and Scarf	Flat Head and Scurf	
Hobnailed Boots	Green Wellies	
Knee-trembler round the back of the Gasworks	Sitting up all Night Discussing the Third Way	

THE LONG WALKIES No.7

My journey by J. Dog Du

Imagine my pride during the General Election campaign of 1997 when I received a special award for having broken the World Record for continuous uninterrupted walkies of 10,000 miles in six weeks!

As well as this I had further cause for satisfaction in that I was able to witness at first hand Chairman Blair's glorious victory and assumption of office. In a very real sense I had become the Ministerial Ro Vaa with my very own Jaa Gwaa.

OUR HEROIC LEADER NO. 7:
MEETING THE MONARCH

THE DOME WILL BE
A BEACON TO THE WORLD

Originally Chairman Blair wanted twin matching Domes complete with architect-designed crack between them, echoing, in a very real sense, that to which all the people should aspire. Ever the realist Chairman Blair soon realised that one large Dome would be a clearer statement of his role as Great Unifier of the Third Way.

As always, Chairman Blair's prescience enabled him to see the fabulous success that our Great Dome at Greenwich would become. On election he was anxious to reaffirm the grandiosity of the Dome and make it a clearer expression of the Third Way. It would be the ultimate monument to The Project of the Third Way. His words at the time bear this out triumphantly:

"Seize the moment and put on something of which we and the world will be proud."

"This is our Dome, Britain's Dome. And believe me, it will be the envy of the world."

"Emotional and uplifting like a West End musical."

"The bandwagon is beginning to roll... Greenwich will be the most exciting place in the world to be."

WOMEN AROUSED: THE BABES OF BLAIR

Chairman Blair realised, after long and careful consideration early in his political career, that but for the contribution of women many of us would not, in fact, be here. Clearly their contribution to society is to be considered as quite important.

As he was later to comment in a fabulously well-received and influential speech to a revolutionary women's organisation:

"When I look at some of the things we have done, the campaigning power of women has played a real role."

This expresses in dramatic fashion the value that Chairman Blair puts on the contribution of women to his Project. This was also shown after the expected but nevertheless fantastic election victory.

Chairman Blair was so grateful to "his" new women MPs that he organised a photo-opportunity just for them.

It was at this deeply significant event that a suitably important name was coined for the women. It was with great rejoicing that a waiting world was told that from now on the old male-dominated ways of Old Labour would be consigned to history. In the future the women would be referred to in a new way, a way which would express the new liberated position they would hold. So it was that "Blair's Babes" came to be their new name.

It is well known that Chairman Blair gets quite excited in the company of women. There is much evidence for this assertion, including this beautiful passage of prose which eloquently raises women to the status of demi-goddesses:

"Look at yourselves... The old image, the old ways, cast off and now dynamic, engaged, socially aware, your slogan: a modern voice for women. You haven't betrayed your past. You've renewed it. So with us, as a nation. We must draw on every ounce of strength in our values, our traditions and our history. The British spirit – determined, fair-minded, gentle but immensely powerful and creative when roused – will be what sees us through. But we do need to be roused."

JOINED-UP THINKING

Too much thought can get in the way of joined-up thinking. Joined-up thinking is the ability thoughtlessly to merge disparate concepts into one significant big idea.

It has been proved that intelligence can be an impediment to joined-up thinking. It is essential when engaging in joined-up thinking always to apply Chairman Blair's thoughts. Only by the relentless and rigorous application of his thoughts can your thought become joined up.

Joined-up writing is joined-up thinking expressed in written form. It is dangerous to use joined-up writing for expressing anything other than joined-up thought. This can lead to false joins.

To clarify, Jon Dog Du writes,"Don't do it, colleagues!"

Verbs are the enemy of joined-up thinking. They are unnecessary appendages that get in the way of true emphasis.

THE CORRECT HANDLING OF THE RED MULLET

The Red Mullet of Social-ism symbolises the significance of New Labour. It complements Chairman Blair's thoughts and can also be wielded to great effect to fend off the massed hordes of the unhelpful press.

1. The Red Mullet should always be depicted as shown.

2. Do not modify the length of the tail or the angle of the dangle.

3. The Red Mullet should be displayed at state occasions and at times of national emergency. It should be run halfway up flagpoles at state funerals.

4. Do not use imitations of the Red Mullet, your own or anybody else's.

5. Always use the approved digitised version of the Red Mullet.

6. The combination of the words "Red" and "Mullet" is a registered trade mark and is supplied to the masses and the media on the condition that they:

(a) Vote for us
(b) Are nice to us

Any adaptation or misuse of the Red Mullet will render the perpetrators liable to swift and merciless punitive

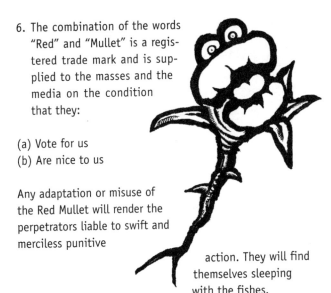

action. They will find themselves sleeping with the fishes.

Further copies of these instructions and a guide to the Red Mullet in action can be obtained free from:
The Fish Counter, Harrods, London.

CHAIRMAN BLAIR'S LESSON No.8

The Responsibility of the Pants of Po Waa

On the glorious morning of Friday May 2nd 1997 Chairman Blair finally pulled on the Pants of Po Waa. As he felt their 100% viscose quality sliding up his thighs he paused mid-pull to give thanks to those who had previously warmed them but been found wanting.

He felt slight revulsion at the thought that only yesterday the infirm and hapless Joh Ma Ja had been occupying these very same pants. But as his mind ranged back in time he was stimulated to think of all the years through which the pants were wielded by his spiritual predecessor, the almost great but ultimately misguided Ma Gra Tha Tcha.

It was enough to give him goose bumps – he was now numero uno, the boss, the man with the responsibility of the Pants of Po Waa. He must wear them with pride but not on his head.

A BETTER CLASS OF PEOPLE

"The Class War is over."

There are two classes in the world: The Under Class and the Better Class. It is axiomatic that the Better Class is better than the Under Class. Thus the Better Class must use all means within its power to make the Under Class better, short of spending any money on it. There must be no compromising of economic realities nor any breaches of correct spending limits.

New Labour is committed to helping the Under Class pull its own socks up with help from selected sponsors in the Private Sector.

THE BETTER CLASS

TOP OF THE RANGE PRODUCTS INSIDE

THIS WAY UP

For those without socks there will be a two socks for the price of three offer available on the internet.

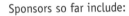

Sponsors so far include:

Banking in the Community (Barclays)

Looking Good on a Tight Budget (Marks & Spencer)

Smoke Yourself Healthy (British American Tobacco)

TOUGH ACTION ON HAIR LOSS

Baldness is just not acceptable in a Modern Social-ist nation. Chairman Blair knows this because he has been blessed with more than his fair share of hair and not just on his head. Much has already be made of Chairman Blair's attraction to the opposite sex. But little has been said about the devastating role played by Chairman Blair's hirsute appearance.

Chairman Blair understands the privilege he has been gifted with and is committed to spreading the benefits of hairiness to the many not the few. Hair is a key component of the Third Way. Hair is, in fact, a Social-ist issue.

It is so important that a whole new slogan was developed: "Tough on Hair Loss and the Causes of Hair Loss." In fact zero tolerance of hair loss. Chairman Blair has set his targets for reducing the waiting list for hair pieces of all kinds including merkins.

No more will the poor pathetic follically challenged have to wait around in dingy corridors for their treatment. Funding to hair clinics will be dramatically increased. This new strategy will attach new growth to the very roots of our society.

One day all members of our hard-working society will stand proudly with the luxuriant hair growth that our leader enjoys.

THE LONG WALKIES No.8

My journey by J. Dog Du

I've always been partial to walnut fascias, and so I was bowled over when our great Chairman Blair himself asked me to be Transport Supremo because this meant I would get my very own walnut fascia with Jaa Gwaa attached.

But even more bowling over was to occur – the job actually came with a pair of Jaa Gwaas, one for me and one to protect the wife's hair. I can tell you I wasted no time in making my mark on each of these magnificent beasts.

EDUCATION
AND THE TRAINING OF PETS

Chairman Blair has strong views on the position of pets in the Third Way. Pets should always remain faithful to the Third Way as expressed in the person of Chairman Blair.

Dogs should bark, but not too much, and bite, but only as directed. They should be given regular walkies and allowed to evacuate as required.

Cats must not scratch members of the inner circle unless bidden to do so by Chairman Blair. Any crapping must always be done in other people's back yards.

Budgerigars and parrots should only speak when spoken to.

Larger pets require special dispensation from Chairman Blair himself. This includes elephants, giraffes and gorillas.

Pets should be educated, educated, educated through thorough training, training, training.

How should this be done?
Three words for dogs: sticks, sticks, sticks.
Three words for cats: fish, fish, fish.

In line with Third Way Thought there are three uses for each of these.

For sticks: throwing, fetching and beating. It is to be admitted that cats sometimes have great difficulty with the fetching of sticks, hence the use of fish.

For fish: throwing, swimming and beating. Dogs sometimes find fish slippery, hence the use of sticks.

Using Chairman Blair's Little Red Book No.4

Political Movement

Posed by models

1. Showing the Books

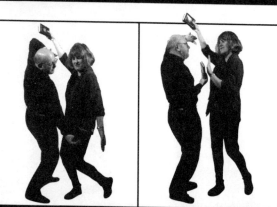

2. Circling the Books

3. Checking the Auras

4. Presenting the Thought   **5. Demonstrating the Thought**

6. Pushing the Thought   **7. Synchronising the Thought**

A DIFFERENT KIND OF NEWNESS

When New Labour swept into power oldness was banished in its current form, probably for ever. It was a turning point in the history of the universe, and was summed up by Chairman Blair's seminal statement which bears repetition here:

"My generation stands at the intersection between old and new."

"In this way the new and old are in harmony. We in Government talk often about the 'new' – whether the 'new' economy, 'new' culture, art, 'new' NHS, 'new' welfare state."

"I know this argument from 'New' Labour. We re-wrote the Party's constitution, changed its policies, altered our rules. We were accused, in doing so, of abandoning our basic values. But I always regarded it as precisely the opposite: that the 'new' was necessary in order to 're-new' the old."

Thus it is possible to deduce that which was hitherto known as "oldness" can be seen, in the light of the Third Way, for what it is – a different kind of newness.

SWEEPING AWAY BOOM AND BUST

Boom and bust was the scourge of our nation until Chairman Blair, in heroic congress with the ever-prudent G'Dong Bru, conquered it for ever. In the future there was to be no boom, no bust. Imagine a world freed from boom and bust for ever and more. A world where nothing could ever boom again, a world where nothing could ever bust again.

Boom and bust gone. They were like thieves in the night but they were rumbled and utterly defeated by the diligent frugality of Chairman Blair and G'Dong Bru, colossuses in the never-ending, never-sleeping battle against the twin evils of boom and bust. They looked those twin evils right in the eye and did not blink.

The easy way, the fool's way would be to boom and bust. But they were not tempted to boom, they were not tempted to bust. They were boomless and bustless and they will remain so for ever. As will a grateful nation and if there is any justice in this twisted modern world New Labour will be in power for ever and ever, world without boom and bust.

"And by 1997 ... and the economy on the way back to the old familiar cycle of boom and bust, we resolved to, and under Chairman Blair, had the strength to take difficult long-term decisions... to protect hard working families from a return to boom and bust... no return to Tory boom and bust... twenty years of boom and bust... avoiding Tory boom and bust."

CHAIRMAN BLAIR'S LESSON No.9

As Chairman Blair's administration matured, like a ripe old cheese it improved with each passing month. The efforts of the many, in the Party and in the country, were piling success upon success. Chairman Blair had always pledged that his government would govern for the benefit of the many, not the few.

But how many were the few and how deserving were the many? These crucial questions had been ignored for too long. It was time to ask the many who they were and how many there were of them, because the only way to make correct policy is to know the facts, and, once the facts are known, to make the policy.

THE PEOPLE'S
SUPREME COMMANDER

As well as being a consummate leader of the nation in peace time, Chairman Blair was soon called on to show his true mettle as a war leader. In conjunction with President Wee Blo Jo of the US of A he continued the heroic secret bombing of the evil empire of I Raq.

Later by his supreme cunning and tactical awareness the beautiful but small forces of Naa Too were able to eliminate the vast and powerful armies of the wildly dangerous Slo Bo Dan.

Here he demonstrated his mastery of smart war – a war without casualties, a war without victims – a truly Holy Third Way War. "What did you do in the Third Way War, daddy?" he was asked by his young daughter. "I won it," Chairman Blair proudly replied.

BUILDING A DOME WITH DILIGENCE AND FRUGALITY

One of the most luminous successes of the early Blair years has been the development of the content of our wonderful Millennium Dome. Trained lackeys scoured Britain for the best and most creative brains to create the stunning, tasteful and relevant contents of the Dome.

Led by the brilliant, mercurial one-eyed trouser snake Man Dee, the Dome crew were always destined to be ultimately successful. Only the whingers and the whiners opposed this wonderfully conceived package of Third Way inspired expression of the state of our nation.

Sadly, before he could see his creation live, Man Dee was unfairly forced to resign because of the furore surrounding the purchase of his stylish new snake pit in London's glamorous Whipsnade district.

THE LONG WALKIES No.9

My journey by J. Dog Du

Chairman Blair had learnt a lot from the tremendous success of rail privatisation where the many were able to travel to more places more reliably and cheaply than at any time in recorded or unrecorded history.

He gave me a new task: faithfully to roll out this fabulous success to all other forms of transport. One of the main planks of this new policy was to develop a Public Private Finance Initiative to improve pedestrian timekeeping, but this would have to wait until the tube and the aeroplanes had been remodelled along Third Way lines.

161

Living a **Third** Way **Day**

1. Clean teeth before waking by chewing wad of floss overnight.
2. Wake up before alarm clock.
3. Clean teeth.
4. 30 minutes violent exercise in lieu of sexual congress.
5. Shower.
6. Clean teeth.
7. Light breakfast of fruit and bran.
8. Clean teeth.
9. Travel to work via ecologically sound transport e.g. solar-powered tram.
10. Otherwise perform vigorous toning exercises in the back of ministerial Jaa Gwaa.*
11. On arrival at place of work, clean teeth. Avoid coffee.
12. Meet with members of inner circle.*
13. Meet with representatives of British Industry, Financial Community or Defence Community.*
14. Make tough decisions.
15. Inform members of Cabinet* of tough decisions.
16. Urge speedy implementation.
17. Avoid coffee and biscuits.
18. Clean teeth.
19. Break for lunch of salad and sparkling mineral water.
20. Clean teeth.
21. Meet with senior Civil Servants.*

NewMullet
NewLabour

22 Make more tough decisions.*

23 Clean teeth.

24 Po Waa Cat Nap (minimum three minutes, maximum seventeen hours).

25 Clean teeth.

26 Eat small but beautifully cooked dinner.

27 Clean teeth.

28 Attend function.*

29 Go home.*

30 Clean teeth.

31 Spend quality time with Red Boxes.*

32 Clean teeth.

33 Spend quality time with yourself.

32 Clean teeth.

33 Sleep (avoid cocoa).

* Or equivalent

The Party understands that not everyone has access to Cabinet colleagues or Leaders of the Business Community. Please fill in your own lifestyle equivalents to make the Third Way your own Way.

THE JU BI LEE HOLE
IN THE GROUND

The Third Way needed something to symbolise its perfection in the public eye. The wonderful Dome went some way towards this but, being only a fabric shell on a remote and polluted South East London peninsula, it required a state-of-the-art hole in the ground to complement it.

This hole in the ground and part-time underground railway was to be called the Third Way Extension Hole in the Ground until a way was found to spread the costs by getting it sponsored. An appropriate sponsor that would help promote the importance of the project was hard to find. But Chairman Blair was overjoyed when Ju Bi Lee Brothers Carpet Sales of Peckham agreed to lend their name – for a consideration of course. The price was agreed at a very reasonable monkey.

The brothers also agreed that the Ju Bi Lee Brothers Carpet Sales of Peckham Hole in the Ground was a bit of a mouthful, and so it was shortened to the Ju Bi Lee Hole in the Ground. In line with Third Way Economics, the main function of the Jubilee Hole in the Ground was to swallow vast amounts of public funding.

According to New Third Way economic thinking, large amounts of money shovelled into holes in the ground across our hard-working nation would eventually benefit a few of the many, not the few, by seeping or trickling up through gaps in the collapsing infrastructure.

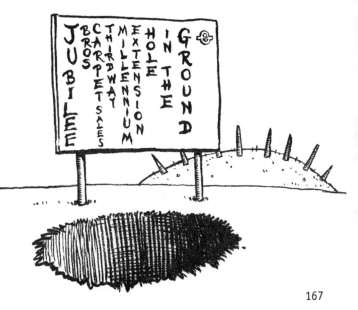

CHAIRMAN BLAIR'S LESSON No.10

Chairman Blair still has tasks to accomplish and infinite potential to achieve. Within his manly grasp are Eternal Power and Life Beyond Death. In the meantime he would be prepared to settle for a Second Term in Office. In order to accomplish this, all he needs to do is to defeat the revisionist forces of the First and Second Ways which are Wee Ham Ha and the pathetic remnants of the Tory Party.

WEE HAM HA

Thus Chairman Blair has decreed that the slogans for the coming campaign shall be:

"Squash The Squit! Lance The Boil!

"Crunch The Ginger Nut of Liberal Democracy!"

CHA KEE BUM

OldLabour	**New**Labour
Smoke-filled Rooms	Smoked Fish-filled Rolls
Northern Grit	Southern Git
Top Shelf Titles	People's Peerages
Redistribution of Wealth	Big Contributions by Stealth
Docker's Leaders	Dot-com Entrepreneurs
Dance at the Palais	Dine at the Palace
Miners and Dockers	Winers and Diners
Closed Shop	24-hour Shopping
Pint in the Snug	Snort in the Club
Red Nose	Red Rose

THE RED FLAG

The people's carrier is deepest blue

It shines so bright when it's been cleaned

I don't do it – I've got a chap for that

He's cheap and doesn't answer back.

CORRECT HANDLING OF CONTRADICTIONS AMONGST THE PEOPLE

When Chairman Blair was elected in 1997 the people were very happy. However, as the new era wore on the atmosphere of intoxicating change and renewal became a little too much for some people. They forgot the truth of the Third Way and began to think selfishly of superficial reasons for discontent with the new conditions.

Contradictions developed – the broad mass of the many were still very happy but a few fat blokes weren't. They needed something but they weren't sure what it was. Would cheaper fish make them happy? Or concreting over the entire South East of England to allow complete access to lorries? Or perhaps they just needed someone to really listen to them. A mate who would always stand next to them in the pub and nod at their every statement, however wild.

So it was that the great Chairman Blair showed us once again his qualities of true leadership. He immediately took command of the situation and coined a new slogan:

"Fat blokes. We feel your pain."

The effect was immediate. All round the country ordinary people spontaneously volunteered to offer their help to local fat blokes. They rushed to every petrol station to offer the fat blokes a transfusion. The cries were heard all through the nation: "Give a Gallon for a Guzzler," and "Free Fuel for Fat Blokes!"

And the Befriend a Fat Bloke scheme went from strength to strength. Every fat bloke was assigned a carer, someone who would be there for him at all the crucial times: in the pub, at B&Q, at football grounds and while out fishing. "Listen to the Fat Blokes," was the cry, and it really made a difference. Happy lorry-loads of friendly fat blokes descended on the nation's capital to show their appreciation of Chairman Blair and his Third Way.

LISTEN TO THE 8 FAT BLOKES

THAT MAN SHOUTED AT MY LORRY!

GESTURE POLITICS

"I'm listening"

"Pensions increase"

"Union leaders"

"I'm telling you"

"Let us pray for a second term"

"What do I think?"

"Hello Dad"

"William 'ague"

"Tony Blair"

"Ow about that!"

178

"But seriously"

"Tony's great"

"I'm no dog"

"Grr!"

THE PRECIOUS RING OF STEEL

Oh! Labour Party
I give you my all
And in return you give me
A brand new ring of steel

A ring around the conference
A ring around Jon Dog Du
A ring around the mullet
A ring around Cha Ree Boo

Oh! Labour Party
I give you my all
And in return you give me
A brand new ring of steel

A ring around the colleagues
A ring around the pier
A ring around the Chairman
Around all that we hold dear

Oh! Labour Party
You're all that I crave
Remember that fortune
Always favours the brave

My dreams all come true
My ills all shall heal
For you have given me
That precious ring of steel

For you have given me
That precious ring of steel.

DRIVING OUT SLEAZE

The dying years of the corrupt and discredited regime of Joh Ma Ja were dominated by a particularly horrid brand of sleaze. All this was driven out when Chairman Blair swept to power. A healing and cleansing process was started that would lead to whole new system of Third Way Ethics.

B E R

N E E

E K

Neither saint nor sinner.

Neither good nor evil.

Not too much.

Not too little.

A little bit of this.

A little bit of that.

Not too much of the other.

This new system of ethics was triumphantly demonstrated in the affair of the munificent and stringless donation from Ber Nee Ek of Fast One plc.

THE LONG WALKIES No.10

My journey by J. Dog Du

The year 2000 saw evil First and Second Way Revisionists seeking to overturn the very real achievements of the Third Way. The ungrateful rail companies, having benefited from the Great Lurch Forward during which they had received more than their due reward, were prominent amongst those whose actions served to detract from the Third Way.

Rather than taking the easy way, the Second Way of sacking these ingrates and appointing someone who knew how to run a railway, I resolved to do it My Way, the Third Way. I vowed to personally commit myself to a World Record-beating long Line Walkies around Britain to check each and every length of rail and to single-handedly replace it where necessary.

RATIONALISING RESOURCES

New Labour believes in delivering election promises. So fervently is this belief held that it insists on even delivering its opponents' election promises. Strangely, this has so far not endeared it either to the opposition or to members of New Labour, proving that there is still much work to be done.

Thus it was that, on succceeding to power, G'Dong Bru scoured the halls and corridors of Westminster for the mythical and long rumoured "Big List of Everything That Isn't Nailed Down" and its appendix, "Everything That Is". This would be the crowning glory of his career and a kind of personal holy grail – the search for the Lost Poond.

Finally, in a dusty cupboard he found the document drafted by his predecessor Wun Fat Blip. It made fascinating reading and sent poond signs flashing across his eyes. He resolved immediately to update it as a matter of national urgency.

The new list, to be called "Quick Ways of Cashing In on the Lost Poond", included the Granny Control Agency, the National Air Supply and the National Soul Repository.

Cynics are fond of claiming that this is simply the Old Tory policy of privatisation by another name. This is absolutely not true. As both Chairman Blair and G'Dong Bru are quick to point out, it is not privatisation at all but a clear and coherent policy of rationalisation of resources.

IS THAT A POOND
IN YOUR POCKET OR
ARE YOU JUST PLEASED
TO SEE ME ?

EQUIPPED FOR POWER

Now you have come to the end of Chairman Blair's Little Red Book you hold in your hand everything you need to lubricate Chairman Blair's passage to eternal power.

If you have read and re-read this book enough times you will be fully equipped to deal with any doubters,

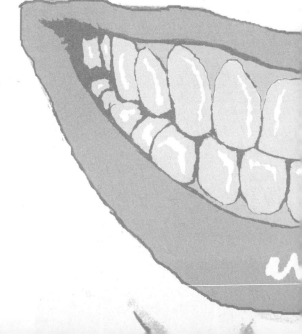

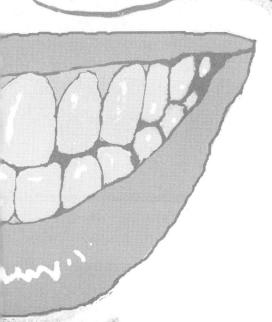

backsliders and sneering cynics. Keep it in your trousers and whip it out whenever necessary to deter enemies of Third Way Thought.

It will also help you keep the Third Way in your heart and enable you to remain forever true to its precepts.

Forward to the Future!

Keep up the good work, colleagues!

Fight the good fight.

Keep **His Thoughts** to the fore and they will last forever.

New**Mullet**
New**Labour**